Building a Lasting Marriage
A Couple's Guide to Happily Ever After

By Sharael Kolberg

ISBN-10: 0988961032 (print)

ISBN-13: 978-0-9889610-3-6 (print)

For Jeff,

After 14 years of marriage, I still get butterflies when I'm with you. Thank you for being the love of my life.

I will always love and adore you!
Share

1. Add Mystery

Strive to continually surprise your spouse with things that are unexpected. It can be as simple as washing his car or buying her a blouse, or as extravagant as planning a surprise weekend away. It's fun to keep your spouse guessing about what you might do next to surprise each other. Why not go all out and send your husband or wife a note to meet you for a cocktail after work and then show up with a wig and an outfit that is totally out of character for you...maybe even speak with a foreign accent! Pretend you are getting to know each other for the first time. Shake things up to keep things interesting.

♥ *Take Action*: What can you do to surprise your spouse? Do something this week to add mystery to your marriage...what about booking a hotel room down the street for a quick overnight get-away or replacing the bulbs in your bedroom lamps with red ones? How about sending your spouse on a romantic scavenger hunt? Have fun with it! Make a list of activities you can do to surprise your spouse and a date that you'll do it on!

Activity:

_____

_____

Date: _____

2. Hold Hands

When you are angry at each other or in an argument, face each other and hold hands. As challenging as it may seem to do while you're upset, it will help you get over your angry feelings quicker. It will be very difficult to stay mad at each other while holding hands and looking into each other's eyes while trying to settling your disagreement. It's also good to hold hands while just talking. It makes the other person feel like you're really listening to them and makes the conversation more meaningful. As a matter of fact, it's also great to hold hands while strolling down the street, sitting on the couch, driving in the car. It's a simple and as meaningful as just touching.

♥ *Take Action*: If you get into an argument or disagreement this week, sit and face each other, hold hands, and try to work it out. If you don't have a disagreement, try holding hands while talking. Focus on being a good listener.

3. Help Others

Get involved with some type of charity. Feed the homeless, help the elderly, plant a tree, be a big brother or sister. It will bring you closer together and make you feel good by helping others. Jeff and I have enjoyed helping Transition Laguna Beach plant edible gardens in residents' yards. Not only were we helping others, but we also made some friends in our community and did something good for the planet. Now's your chance to make a difference in the world and get closer to your spouse (and meet some amazing people) while doing something good. Even if all you can do is take time to clean your closet and donate your clothes to Goodwill, anything helps.

♥ *Take Action*: Do some research to find a charity that you'd like to volunteer for. What do you care most about...rescuing animals, feeding those in need, building homes for the homeless? There are plenty of organizations that could use an extra hand to help those less fortunate. Don't miss out on this opportunity. Check out the website www.volunteermatch.org.

List charities that you're interested in:

1. _____

2. _____

3. _____

4. _____

4. Don't Change

Realize that you cannot change the person you married into something they're not. You need to accept your differences if you're going to have a successful marriage. Opposites often attract, but then they try to change the things about each other that are not the same as they are. Think how boring it would be to be married to someone that has the same thoughts and views as you do. Celebrate your differences. Learn from each other. Your differences can help each of you grow and see things from a different perspective. Do whine about what's different about your spouse. Don't try to fix him or her. Learn to live with your differences. Celebrate your own individuality and uniqueness!

♥ *Take Action*: How can you learn from your partner? Does she enjoy yoga? Does he enjoy riding motorcycles? Choose one thing to learn from each other this week. Express to your spouse why you are the way you are. Maybe he or she hasn't seen things from your point of view. Maybe you could each grow as individuals by incorporating each other's hobbies or habits. Be open-minded and you might just be surprised and learn something new about your spouse.

5. Be Committed

Being married means that you are committed to each other, no matter what...through thick and thin, good and bad, sickness and health. You must be faithful and put that person first in your life. People make mistakes, things won't always be perfect, but you need to learn to forgive and forget. No matter how bad things get, you must be willing to give that person the benefit of the doubt and forgive them when they make mistakes. Being committed means being honest, open, intimate, loyal, devoted, and loving someone unconditionally. You have to be willing to work through you problems and stick it out. You will do whatever it takes to make it work.

♥ *Take Action*: Has your spouse done something

that has made you bitter or angry? Tell them you

forgive them and that you're committed to making the

marriage work, no matter what. Write each other a

note promising your love to each other no matter

what. Reassure your spouse that you are deeply

committed to the relationship.

6. Be Best Friends

Above all else, you must be best friends. Not only are you husband and wife, as well as lovers, but true friends. If you had the opportunity to go to an event, whom would you want to go? You should always want to be with your spouse above anyone else. It doesn't mean that you spend all of your time with your spouse. You should also make time for friends and family, but your spouse should be the person that you most enjoy spending your time with. Romance will come and go at different times in your relationship, but the friendship is what will keep your relationship strong. Think of things you can do to build your friendship with your spouse. It shouldn't be hard. There must be things you enjoy doing together.

♥ *Take Action*: Come up with a list of friendship

activities you can do together...see a movie, go

shopping, have lunch. Put it on the calendar and do it!

What activities would you enjoy doing together?

1. _____

2. _____

3. _____

4. _____

5. _____

6. _____

7. _____

8. _____

9. _____

10. _____

11. _____

7. A Secret Sign

Find a way to communicate to each other that you love each other or are thinking of each other without saying a word. Whether it's a hand gesture, a special wink, or a secret word...it's playful to have this way of communicating, especially when in a crowd. When Jeff and I were getting married, we were standing at the alter and he squeezed my hand three times (our way of saying "I love you" without words). It calmed my nerves and brought a big smile to my face. I knew he was the right one for me. I squeezed his hand back four times (our way of saying "I love you too"). Having a secret way of showing your love can be fun and flirtatious. Give it a try!

♥ *Take Action*: Come up with a secret way of communicating with your spouse. It will come in handy more often than you would think. You don't have to limit yourself to just one secret way of communicating. You can text a "kiss" emoticon, come up with an entire secret language with several words that have alternate meanings, give each other Hershey kisses. What are your ideas to show your love?

1. _____

2. _____

3. _____

4. _____

5. _____

6. _____

7. _____

8. A Year to Cherish

The first year of marriage is the time when you really should work on strengthening your bond with each other and learn as much about each other as you can. If you put a lot of energy and effort into building a strong marriage the first year, it will be smooth sailing from then on. Put time into your marriage and work on building a strong foundation. If you've already been married for more than a year, consider taking a year to purely focus on your marriage. Try not to undertake anything that is extremely time consuming during that year, like going back to school, buying a house, or starting a business. Try to focus on your marriage by spending time together. Make your marriage your first priority.

♥ *Take Action*: Make a written contract that you will not take on anything that will take the focus away from your first year of marriage. Sign and date it!

"I _____ will commit to put our marriage first this year. This means that I will not put work (if possible), hobbies, friends, or family before my spouse for this entire year of marriage. I look forward to having this time to build a stronger bond with my spouse and show that my marriage is my number one priority."

Signature: _____

Date: _____

9. Set Goals

Like anything you do in life, you must set goals to achieve what you want. Marriage is the same way. You need to set goals to achieve what you want out of marriage. You should write a vision statement of what your idea of an ideal marriage is. This will help you to define your goals, values, and direction for your marriage. Your vision could include categories such as finances, spiritual, friends, family, community, career, education, hobbies, health & wellness, philanthropy. There are always things that can be improved. Work towards having the perfect marriage, one step at a time. Do you want to buy a house a year from now? Do you want to have kids five years form now? These are things you should discuss and plan for.

♥ *Take Action*: Make time to write your vision statement. Be specific. Set goals for one year, five years, and ten years. Where would you like to be at those times in your marriage?

Goals for one year:

_____

_____

Goals for five years:

_____

_____

Goals for ten years:

_____

_____

10. Have Fun

Make time to have fun together. Don't get stuck in a rut. Take time to do things together that make you laugh...take a class together, find a hobby that you both enjoy, go to a comedy club, take a trip somewhere, go for a hike, join a sports team. Jeff and I love snow skiing together in Mammoth Lakes. We chase each other down the slopes, hold hands on the chairlift and just laugh. What do each of you enjoy doing? Whether it's taking a pottery class, planting a garden, paddling a kayak on the weekends, wine tasting, baking cookies, or just going dancing, be sure to keep that spark alive by doing something fun on a regular basis. Think outside the box and find things you've never tried.

♥ *Take Action*: What fun activity can you do together? Make a list. Write one activity on your calendar this week. Don't cancel!

Activity Ideas:

1. _____

2. _____

3. _____

4. _____

5. _____

6. _____

7. _____

8. _____

9. _____

10. _____

11. Take Ten

Try to take ten minutes every day to talk to each other. You each get five minutes of uninterrupted time (no butting in). I know that ten minutes doesn't sound like much time, but when you're busy with work, doing laundry, exercising, it sometimes seems difficult to take even ten minutes out of your hectic schedule to really talk with your spouse. Take the time to share your thoughts and feelings with your spouse. You might not want to use this time to talk about how your day was, because you will normally find time to do that. This time should be spent really sharing your feelings and thoughts about your relationship or hopes and dreams for your future. Discuss things that your wouldn't normally take the time to talk about.

♥ *Take Action*: Take ten minutes every day to talk

to each other this week. Start making it a habit! Not

only are you talking, but sincerely listening too.

12. Monthly Anniversary

It's nice to remember the day you got married. It makes you cherish the love you have. Take the time to do something special every month on the day of the month you got married. Have a glass of champagne, light some candles, go out to dinner, take a walk, watch the sunset, dance to your wedding song, flip through your wedding album or watch your wedding video. Just take a moment to remember why you married your spouse and what you love about him or her. Re-reading your wedding vows is a powerful way to reiterate your commitment to each other. Take the time to rekindle the spark that attracted you to each other in the first place. Cherish the marriage you have.

♥ *Take Action*: This week schedule time together on your anniversary day. Decide how you'll celebrate the special day. Make plans and put it on your calendar.

What day of the month did you get married on?

_____

What will you do to celebrate your marriage? Be creative, be elaborate, keep it simple...whatever works for you!

_____

_____

_____

_____

_____

_____

13. Be Romantic

Keep romance alive. Have candlelight dinners, take a bubble bath together, buy some sexy lingerie, watch a sunset, go on a picnic, write love notes to each other, buy flowers, or give each other a massage. I still remember when Jeff and I were first married and he surprised me by taking me to a bench over looking Ocean Beach in San Francisco. He pulled out a bottle of champagne and a single rose. It was a simple, but meaningful gesture that I cherished. Being romantic takes work. You have to really try to be romantic, it won't just happen on it's own. But it is worth it. Your spouse will truly appreciate the effort. If you're not sure how to be romantic, do some research...it's not as hard as you might think!

♥ *Take Action*: What romantic activity can you do this week? Be creative. Be committed to doing it! You'll be glad you did. Candles, roses, and chocolates go a long way.

List your romantic ideas and put them into action:

1. _____

2. _____

3. _____

4. _____

5. _____

6. _____

7. _____

8. _____

9. _____

14. Date Night

Once you get married, you might not make as much time for "dates" anymore. For some reason that seems to be something you do when your dating and it can fade away once you get married. Set aside one night each week (or once a month, if nothing else) to focus on your relationship. This is your chance to show how important your relationship is to each other and take time to focus on each other rather than to-do lists or work obligations. Make the date fun, interesting and memorable. How about a candlelit dinner at home, a drive-in movie, roller-skating, a walk in the woods, a sunset sail? Do something you both enjoy and have fun doing it.

♥ *Take Action*: Decide which night of the week (or month) you will dedicate to a date night. Come up with some fun things you'd like to do together for your special night out and make a date to do it.

Night of the week or month: _____

Date Night Ideas:

    1. _____

    2. _____

    3. _____

    4. _____

    5. _____

    6. _____

    7. _____

15. Your Marriage Comes First

Your relationship should be a first priority in your lives. It should come before your families, before your friends, before your hobbies and extracurricular activities, and even before your job (if possible). This is one of the most important things you can do for your relationship. Put each other first and you won't regret it. Rather than surfing an extra hour, head home to be with your spouse. Instead of working an hour later, spend time with your spouse. When you have an option, you should try to make your spouse feel as though they are the priority in your life. Once you say, "I do," you need to be mindful of your spouse rather than yourself.

♥ *Take Action*: Write and sign a contract to put

your spouse first – above all else.

Here's an example:

"I promise to put you _____, above all

else in my life because you mean the world to me and

I want to make you my number one priority. I am so

happy to be married to you and want you to know

that you will always come first. Whenever possible, I

will choose you above work, hobbies, friends and

family. I love spending time with you and cherish our

time together.

I love you,

_____ "

16. Be Independent

Even though you are in a relationship with your spouse, don't forget who you are. Make sure to continue to do things that you enjoy on your own. Set personal goals for yourself and nourish your personal growth. It's attractive to be confident and self-fulfilled, rather than needy. Allow each other some "alone time" to get in touch with yourselves. Support your spouse and his or her individual endeavors. Your spouse will thank you and you will both be proud of each other's accomplishments. Make time for a favorite hobby, train for a competitive athletic event, pursue a higher education. Whatever it is, cherish who you are as an individual!

♥ *Take Action*: Schedule some alone time this week. Use this time to do something you enjoy...read a book, go for a bike ride, get a manicure. What are your personal goals? What would you like to accomplish? Learn a language? Become a chef? Make a list of what you enjoy and what you'd like to accomplish and start working towards those objectives.

Individual Goals:

1. _____

2. _____

3. _____

4. _____

5. _____

6. _____

17. Take Control

Remember that you are in control of your own happiness. Don't let your spouse (or anyone else) determine your happiness. You need to be comfortable with who you are. You are in control of your feelings. Sometimes it's easy to become codependent on your spouse and to let the way they treat you or the way they act towards you affect the way you feel. But no matter how someone else treats you, it's up to you how you respond to his or her treatment. If your husband doesn't buy you flowers, are you going to mope around the house feeling sorry for yourself? Or are you going to go to the store and buy your own flowers? Make yourself happy; don't rely on someone else to make you happy.

♥ *Take Action*: If your spouse does something that makes you unhappy this week – take matters into your own hands and make yourself happy. Do something this week that makes you happy rather than depending on your spouse. Fulfill your own needs. Don't depend on someone else to do it.

What makes you happy?

1. _____

2. _____

3. _____

4. _____

5. _____

6. _____

18. Support Each Other

Times are not always going to be good. You need to be there for each other, especially when things are bad -- that is when your spouse will need the most comforting. Whether it's a job loss, the passing of a relative, or financial challenges, your spouse is going to need you there to listen and offer support. Maybe he or she won't want your advice, but I guarantee that they'll want an ear to listen and maybe a shoulder to cry on. Even though you might have a million things that need to be done, you need to stop what you're doing and take the time to be there for your spouse in time of need. You need to try not to be judgmental. Show your unconditional love.

♥ *Take Action*: If your spouse needs comforting or support this week – be there for him or her by being a good listener. Don't try to offer advice or come up with solutions.

19. Inspire Each Other

We all have dreams that we'd like to achieve. It's that much easier to strive to achieve them with support from your spouse. Inspire each other to make your dreams come true. When I was trying to become a writer, I didn't have a car at the time so my husband Jeff would drive me wherever I needed to go to interview people for my articles. I truly believe I could not have gotten where I am without his support. Encourage each other to achieve your dreams. If you believe in your spouse, they might believe in themselves more. It's amazing how much it means to have someone you love be proud of you. It can be a great motivator. Being a support spouse will make your marriage stronger.

♥ *Take Action*: Both of you write a list of your dreams or things you'd like to accomplish. Share these lists with each other.

What are your dreams?

1. _____
2. _____
3. _____

What can you do to support your spouse's dreams?

1. _____
2. _____
3. _____
4. _____
5. _____

20. Walk in Their Shoes

If you are having a disagreement with your spouse, try very hard to see things from his or her perspective. I know it's not easy to do when you're upset or angry, but if you can step back and try to understand the way he or she feels or what their true motive was, it might give you a better understanding of where he or she is coming from. Don't worry about who's right or wrong. Be open-minded and try to understand your spouse's point of view. Give him or her the benefit of the doubt. By walking in someone else's shoes, you might realize that the disagreement you are having is really now worth arguing about after all.

♥ *Take Action*: If you have a disagreement with your spouse this week, rather than being defensive, honestly try to see his or her side of things and give him or her some leeway in order to resolve the conflict more quickly. After all, you will probably not even remember what you were arguing about three months from now anyway.

21. Exceed Expectations

Sit down and ask your spouse what they want and need from your relationship. Don't expect each other to read each other's mind. Once you realize what he or she wants, try exceeding his or expectations. Your spouse will be pleased that you care so much about his or her needs. It is one of the best ways to show you care. For example, when my husband Jeff goes out of town on business, he always call me BEFORE I even have the chance to wonder why he hasn't called. Exceeding someone's expectations is a wonderful surprise. If you do things before your spouse asks you to, it means so much more. If your spouse has to ask you to do something, then they'll think you only did it because they asked you to, and that it wasn't sincere.

♥ *Take Action*: Make a list of what you want or need from your relationship. Exchange lists. What can you do this week to fulfill one of these wants or needs?

What do you want from your spouse?

1. _____

2. _____

3. _____

4. _____

5. _____

6. _____

7. _____

8. _____

9. _____

22. Greetings

Kissing is one way of showing your spouse that you love him or her. One thing that I have found is meaningful is to always kiss your spouse hello and goodbye. Whether he or she is just going to the grocery store, to work for the entire day, or out of town for a week, kiss goodbye. Even if they just left and return in only a few minutes, kiss hello. It might seem like a bit much, but I guarantee you it will keep you close, put a smile on your face and might even make you laugh at times. It's a wonderful ritual. And don't forget to kiss good morning and good night! Just a peck on the lips is all it takes, but make sure to also make time for longer, more sensual kisses too!

♥ *Take Action*: Kiss your spouse hello and

goodbye and good morning and good night every day

this week.

23. Don't Go To Bed Angry

If at all possible, try to resolve your differences before going to bed for the night. It's a good motivator to settle your arguments in a timely manner. You have got to resolve things eventually, and it doesn't help to go to bed mad. All that will happen is that you will sleep poorly and wake up bitter towards your spouse because you didn't get any sleep. Why toss and turn when you don't need to? It doesn't matter who is "right." Get over it. Suck it up and make time to work out your problems before your heads hit the pillow. You'd be surprised how much a good snuggle will resolve your conflicts. Make it a point to never sleep on the couch.

♥ *Take Action*: If you have an argument, make sure to work it out and kiss and makeup before bedtime. Promise to never go to sleep in separate locations when angry.

24. Early Bird

Are you an early riser and he likes to sleep in? Do you like to make love in the morning and your spouse likes to make love at night? Having different schedules can make things difficult, but you can't expect the other person to change their habits to accommodate you. What you can do is be flexible. If your honey wants to sleep in, let him. Don't wake him just because you want to get up and start your day. Instead, enjoy some peace and quiet to yourself in the mornings. But also make an effort to sleep in with your love once in a while and enjoy a good snuggle. You need to compromise. It might be enlightening to do things on his or her schedule once in a while. You might even find that you like to sleep in.

♥ *Take Action*: Take turns trying each other's schedules together this week. It's good to vary your routine and try something different. Get up together, work out together, watch a favorite show together...you get the picture.

25. Sweet Dreams

If you have different schedules, still try to go to bed together at the same time, even if it means that you stay up in bed and read while he falls asleep. Sure, it's easy to be lured into staying up later to watch your favorite TV show or catch up on that pile of emails in your inbox. Going to bed together can be an important bonding moment. Sometimes you might not have time in your day to catch up with each other, but you will often tell each other your thoughts or things on your mind before drifting off to sleep while holding each other close. To be held while falling asleep can be so comforting. Don't deny yourselves the bonding moment.

♥ *Take Action*: Make it a point to go to bed together every night at the same time this week. Try to make it a habit. Agree on a time to hit the hay. Consider buying some super soft sheets, a fluffy duvet, and comfy pillows to make bedtime extra luring.

26. Lighten Up

Do you occasionally tease each other? Try not to take things too personally. Your spouse is probably only trying to be playful and not intending to hurt your feelings anyway. Lighten up and learn to laugh at yourself. Laugh at your faults. Don't be so hard on yourself. You don't need to be perfect! Don't worry so much about what other people think of you. You'll probably realize that what someone is teasing you about is not really a big deal after all. Don't dwell on it. Let it go and move on without giving it another thought. Life is much more enjoyable if you're easy going and can learn to laugh at yourself. You'll be much more attractive and enjoyable to be around.

♥ *Take Action*: If your spouse teases you about something this week, try not to take it personally. Try to laugh it off. If it really does hurt your feelings though, let him know. He probably doesn't realize it upsets you so much.

27. Annoying Habits

I guarantee you that your spouse has some annoying habit that drive you crazy. The best thing that you can do is sit down with your spouse and honestly share your concern, without being angry, without blaming your spouse and without nagging him or her. If you nag him or her about it, your souse is likely to get defensive and not do what you ask. If, after talking with your spouse sincerely and calmly, your spouse still doesn't stop the annoying behavior, then let it go. Try not to let it bother you. Just think of all of the wonderful things that your spouse does. You'll probably realize that you can live with the annoying habit after all.

♥ *Take Action*: Take time this week to talk calmly about each other's annoying habits. Does he leave his dirty laundry all over the floor? Does she leave her dirty dishes in the sink? Share your thoughts and work on changing those habits to create a more peaceful household...or learn to live with it.

What habits bother you?

_____

_____

_____

How can you compromise?

_____

_____

28. It's a Privilege

Remember that being married to your spouse is a privilege and an honor. Out of all the people in the world, he or she chose to be married to you! Don't take that for granted. Always cherish the fact that you found each other and have built a loving relationship with each other. There are many people your age that are still single, divorced or widowed. You should be grateful to be in a loving, committed relationship. Remember how wonderful your spouse is and how lucky you are to be married to that special person. Take time to stop and realize that your relationship is something to cherish. Be thankful for what you have and remember to find joy in your marriage.

♥ *Take Action*: Make a list of things that you enjoy about your spouse. Put this list somewhere you can see it every day so you don't take them for granted.

What I enjoy most about my spouse is:

1. _____

2. _____

3. _____

4. _____

5. _____

6. _____

7. _____

8. _____

9. _____

10. _____

29. Compliment Each Other

You may know that your spouse finds you attractive or thinks that you are intelligent, kind, or patient, but it's always nice to hear it. Compliment your spouse as often as you can, as long as it's sincere. What do you love about your spouse? Does she have beautiful eyes or make the best cookies you've ever tasted? Do you like his sense of style or the fact that he always opens to door for you? Tell him or her. Thank him or her for the qualities that you love about him or her. Is he a wonderful father or loving husband? Do you think he is sexy or admire his motivation? Be sure to take the time to tell your spouse what you love about him or her on a regular basis. Saying, "I love you," is the biggest compliment of all.

♥ *Take Action*: Make a list of things you can

compliment your spouse on and try hard this week to

compliment him or her as often as you can.

1. _____

2. _____

3. _____

4. _____

5. _____

6. _____

7. _____

8. _____

9. _____

10. _____

11. _____

30. Wish List

Make a wish list. Tell each other specifically what types of things the other person could do that would bring a smile to your face. Tell him or her things you'd like to do together or what you'd like out of the relationship. Things on a wish list might include going for walks at sunset, receiving flowers, working out together, giving each other a good morning kiss. I remember one thing on Jeff's wish list was that we workout together. Seeing his list made me want to prioritize what he found important for our relationship. We ended up training and completing a marathon together. It was such an amazing way to bond. Each week we had time to do an activity together while working towards a goal.

♥ *Take Action*: Make a wish list at least once a year. It's a great way to tell each other what you want or need. And it's so much fun fulfilling someone else's wishes. Fulfill something on each other's wish list this week.

What do you wish to receive from your spouse or your relationship?

1. _____

2. _____

3. _____

4. _____

5. _____

6. _____

7. _____

31. Couple's Journal

Writing is such a wonderful way to express your feelings and having things written down is a great moment to look back on. Make a couple's journal to share your thoughts with each other. Choose a topic and each of you write down what your thoughts are on that topic and then share with each other. Put these pages in a binder to reflect on at a later time. Some topics for your journal might include things like what are you most afraid of, what's your best childhood memory, where would you like to travel to? Come up with thought provoking questions that really help you get to know each other. It's a great way to spend some quality time together.

♥ *Take Action*: Buy a journal and some nice pens this week and set aside some time to write in the journal together.

Here are some questions to get you started:

- What would you do with a million dollars?

- What country would you most like to visit?

- What are you most scared of?

- What would you like to do before you die?

- What's your favorite memory?

- What are you most proud of?

- What's your most embarrassing moment?

- Who has had the biggest influence on your life?

- What motivates you?

32. Turn the Television Off

Sometimes its' so easy, after a long work day, to just come home and do something brainless, like watching TV. Often it's a great way to relax after a stressful day on the job, but it's easy to get into the habit of watching TV rather than spending quality time together. Turn the TV off and do something more interactive at least once a week. You'd be amazed how much time TV can zap from your relationship. Make an effort not to let it become a daily habit to come home and turn on the TV as soon as walking in the door. The next thing you'll know it'll be time for bed and you might not have said two words to each other. That goes for the Internet too. Don't get sucked into checking email, Facebook or Instagram.

♥ *Take Action*: Make it a habit to have some non-TV time this week. Try some old school activities like doing a puzzle, baking cookies, or playing Jenga.

List some thing you can do at home together instead of watching TV:

1. _____

2. _____

3. _____

4. _____

5. _____

6. _____

7. _____

8. _____

9. _____

33. Pet Names

It's amazing how just calling someone Honey or Sweetie can make him or her feel so special. It may seem so silly, but pet names are a surprisingly powerful way to make each other feel loved. If you always call your loved one Honey, surprise him or her with a new pet name. It's guaranteed to make him or her smile. Jeff has so many pet names for me that my bridesmaids included them in their toast at our wedding! He's still coming up with new ones. It's very endearing. Pet names are a personal way to make someone feel special and loved. Try to come up with a name that has meaning...the sappier the better. Give it a try!

♥ *Take Action*: Start calling your spouse by a new pet name this week. Here are some generic examples: Honey, Love, Baby, Snookum, Cupcake, Pumpkin, Dear...or try to come up with something that is more meaningful. This is meant to be silly, not serious.

Possible Pet Names:

1. _____

2. _____

3. _____

4. _____

5. _____

6. _____

7. _____

8. _____

34. Serenade Each Other

When is the last time you sang to your spouse? Never? Why not give it a try? Sing him or her a lullaby when going to sleep. Sing them a love song while dancing in your living room. Sing to him or her in the shower. Go to a karaoke bar and sing a duet together...any song from "Grease" is bound to be a good choice! You don't need to have a good voice. Don't be afraid to sing sweet nothings to the one you love. It's fun and will probably end up making both of you laugh. Too shy to sing in person? Why not record your song and play it back to him or her on your computer. That still counts! You're guaranteed to earn some brownie points for singing your heart out.

♥ *Take Action*: Pick a favorite song and sing to your spouse this week.

35. Spice Up Your Sex Life

Sex is a very important part of your marriage. Not only is it a way to show each other you love each other, but it's also a great stress reliever and a way to have fun together. It's the most intimate thing you can do. Some married couples still make love, but lose some of the passion after a while. Don't let that happen to you! Be adventurous with your sex life. Try different positions, read books, buys some sexy lingerie. Sometimes it might be difficult to be in the mood after a long day at work, but you really need to make an effort to try to keep your sex life exciting. Don't ever let it get routine. It's amazing how much doing this will keep your relationship fresh and new, even after years of marriage.

♥ *Take Action*: Make a list of things you can do to spice up your sex life. Watch a porno, buy some massage oil, or invest in some sex toys. Choose one to do this week!

1. _____

2. _____

3. _____

4. _____

5. _____

6. _____

7. _____

8. _____

9. _____

10. _____

11. _____

36. Take Ten

Sometimes when you're in a disagreement, you may get so angry that you lose all perspective and just say things you don't mean because you are being defensive. At these times it might be best to just walk away and reschedule the discussion for another time. Don't ignore the issue, rather just talk about it at a time when you've had a chance to cool down. It's better than saying or doing things you might regret. Be very specific and set a date and time when to continue the discussion, even if it is just ten minutes later. How ever long it takes for you to calm down, but don't postpone it for more than 24 hours. It's best to resolve things as quickly as you can.

♥ *Take Action*: The next time you have an

argument and you are too angry to solve the problem,

reschedule it for later. Give yourself time to cool down

so you don't do or say anything irrational and regret it

later.

37. There Is No Mr. Right

The concept of finding a "Mr. Right" seems like a great idea. We've all dreamed of finding the perfect person to spend the rest of our lives with...our prince in shining armor. But when people are in a relationship that isn't going well, it's easy to say, "Well, he must not have been the 'one'." The truth is, there is no such thing as a perfect relationship. Mr. Right does not exist. Everyone has flaws. The sooner you realize that, the better off you'll be. Marriage is not like the fairytales, it takes work. You can't just give up when it's not ideal. Until you decide to put the effort it takes into making it work, you'll always end up with Mr. Wrong.

♥ *Take Action*: Make a list of the things you adore about your spouse. Focus on those things and realize that if you're willing to work at it, you don't need Mr. Right because the one you have is the Right one for you! Share your list with your spouse.

My spouse is the perfect match for me because:

1. _____

2. _____

3. _____

4. _____

5. _____

6. _____

7. _____

8. _____

9. _____

38. Split the Chores

It's a good idea to divvy up the chores so that you don't expect each other to do them and so you don't get bitter towards each other if one person ends up doing them more often. For example, one of you can be responsible for taking out the trash one week and the other person can be responsible for doing the dishes, then the next week you can swap. Or, you can each do specific chores each week. Jeff usually takes out the trashcans each week. I usually do the grocery shopping. We both do laundry. If you share the responsibility you will me less likely to feel overburdened by the housework and thankful to have someone to share the responsibility with.

♥ *Take Action*: Make a chore chart. Write down the weekly chores and who's responsible for doing what. Hang it on the frig. This will prevent any arguing about who was supposed to do what and serve as a reminder as to what your in charge of doing.

Here is list of possible chores:

- Pay the bills

- Do the laundry

- Put the dishes in the dishwasher

- Take out the trash

- Vacuum

- Dust

- Go grocery shopping

39. Be a Kid Again

When is the last time you played on a swing, built a sandcastle, ate Jell-O, ran through the sprinklers, flew a kit, or painted with finger paints? Just because you're getting older doesn't mean you have to forget about the kid in you. Set aside some "playtime" with your spouse. Put your adult responsibilities aside just for a moment and enjoy some good, clean fun. Sure, it's going to feel unnatural, but that's OK. Just go with it. It's liberating to let the kid in you come out and play. Be spontaneous, be silly, don't hold back, laugh, have fun. Don't forget to pack a peanut butter and jelly sandwich for lunch and put naptime in the schedule.

♥ *Take Action*: Schedule some playtime this week...play hopscotch, shoot hoops, build a fort. Share childhood memories over a cup of hot cocoa.

List some ideas you can do together to bring out the child in each of you:

1. _____

2. _____

3. _____

4. _____

5. _____

6. _____

7. _____

8. _____

40. Get Healthy Together

One of the best things you can do as a couple is to get healthy together. Inspire each other to eat better by taking a healthy cooking class together, going grocery shopping for healthy foods together, preparing healthy meals together. Why not start off by training for a 5K race? Who knows, you might end up doing a marathon together. Being fit and healthy shows respect for your body, gratitude for your life, reduces stress, and makes you feel and look good. Why not engage in this lifelong goal as a couple? You might even meet other couples that share your same zest for a long and healthy life and enjoy their company along your journey.

♥ *Take Action*: What goals can you set to start working towards being healthy together? What exercise might you enjoy doing as a couple? How can you improve your eating habits? How can you support each other? Start small...take baby steps. You don't have to change your lives overnight. Just don't wait another minute...start right now! Life is way too short.

1. _____

2. _____

3. _____

4. _____

5. _____

6. _____

7. _____

8. _____

41. Create a Budget

A big source of contention for many couples can be money. It is most often what leads to arguments...not having enough money, spending too much money, spending money on the wrong types of items. In an effort to keep the peace, one of the most important things you can do as a couple is to create a financial budget. Does she want to spend $500 a month on clothes? Does he want to plan a lavish trip to Cabo? By coming to an agreement on how you want to spend your money as a couple, you will avoid any surprises when bills arrive. It doesn't mean you'll stick to the budget all of the time, but it will give you a good point of reference to see what both of you are comfortable with when it comes to making purchases.

♥ *Take Action*: List items for your budget and how much you'd like to spend on a monthly basis. Here are a few things you might want to include:

1. Rent/Mortgage: $_____

2. Utilities: $_____

3. Gas: $_____

4. Groceries: $_____

5. Car payments: $_____

6. Car insurance: $_____

7. Gym membership: $_____

8. Entertainment: $_____

9. Dining out: $_____

10. Clothes: $_____

11. Cell phone: $_____

12. Wi-Fi: $_____

13. Travel: $_____

14. Cable TV: $_____

42. Relax

Take the time to de-stress yourself. You'll be more enjoyable to be around if you practice some stress relieving techniques. Whether it's meditation, yoga, going for a run, listening to soothing music, taking a bubble bath or having a glass of wine, try to find a way to lower any stress you might have. You will be less irritable, more easy-going and probably easier to get along with, which is always good for a relationship. For Jeff and I, spending time with our dog Charlie is a big stress reliever for us. We enjoy taking him for a walk, petting his soft fur, or having him curl up on our lap. You can de-stress on your own or together as a couple, whatever fits your schedule.

♥ *Take Action*: Take time to de-stress this week. Make a list of relaxing activities you enjoy and do one of them. While doing it, focus on how good it feels so that you will hopefully want to do a relaxing activity much more often. It is not a luxury; it is a necessity for a healthy mind, body and marriage!

1. _____

2. _____

3. _____

4. _____

5. _____

6. _____

7. _____

8. _____

9. _____

43. Old Married Couple

Just because you're married doesn't mean you have to become an "old married couple." You can still go out dancing until the wee hours or go to a rock concert or party with your friends. Once you get married, you might find that you prefer spending a nice quiet evening at home with your spouse rather than going bar hopping with your friends until 4 a.m. But although your lifestyle will change for the most part, it doesn't mean that you should never do these things anymore. Make it a point to still enjoy doing some of the things you did when you were single, except picking up on members of the opposite sex, of course. Why not do a weekend away with the girls? Or have a poker night with the guys?

♥ *Take Action*: Enjoy a night out on the town with your friends or go on a double date with another couple this week.

44. See a Counselor

Even if you are getting along perfectly, it's still a great idea to schedule regular appointments with a marriage counselor. By doing this you are really making an appointment to spend time with your spouse, focusing on your relationship. Sometimes our lives get so busy that we don't make time to talk about how our marriage is doing. Meeting with a counselor is really time for you to assess where things are at and make some tweaks if necessary. It's very powerful to have someone to talk to that is unbiased. It will definitely help you to see things from your spouse's perspective and help you work through any rough spots before they become potholes.

Take Action: Find a couple's counselor and set up a meeting this week. Tell the counselor if you have any issues you need to work through. If not, ask for relationship-building advice. Make regular appointments for every three months or less. If nothing else, it's just a good time to just check in with each other and make sure you're on the right path towards keeping your marriage strong and everlasting.

45. Gift day

Pick one day out of the month to surprise each other with some sort of gift. It can be your anniversary day, the night of a full moon, or the first Saturday of the month, just pick a day that has some sort of meaning (and is easy to remember) and make that Gift Day. Put it on your calendar! The gift doesn't have to be lavish or expensive. It can be as simple as a love letter or a single rose. It's the thought that counts. It's nice to know that your spouse is thinking of you and it's great to have a chance to spoil your love with some token of affection. You'll love the anticipation of receiving your gift! If you really enjoy this, you might want to do it once a week!

♥ *Take Action*: Choose a gift day for this month. Pick out a gift this week that you'll give to your spouse on gift day.

Our gift day will be on: _____

Some ideas for gifts:

1. Flowers

2. A massage (from you!)

3. Earrings

4. A framed photo of the two of you

5. A car wash

6. A bottle of wine

7. Clothing

8. A nice dinner

46. Professional Portraits

Make an appointment with a professional photographer to have your portraits taken together. It's a nice activity to do once a year. Don't do it in a studio. Standing and posing for the camera is no fun. Do one of your favorite activities and have the photographer document it or pick a favorite spot that has meaning for you both. Do you enjoy horseback riding or going to the beach? Have your photo taken while riding together on a horse or frolicking in the ocean. This doesn't have to be serious. Have fun with it. You're not only taking photos, you're making memories. You'll be glad to have these photos to look back on as your relationship matures.

♥ *Take Action*: Schedule a photo session with your spouse this week. If you can't afford a professional photographer, have a friend take the photos.

Our portrait session:

Name of the photographer:

_____

Phone number:

_____

Date _____

Time _____

47. Appreciate Each Other

Whenever your spouse does something nice for you, be sure to let him or her know how much you appreciate it. If you take things for granted, then your spouse might stop making the effort. There's nothing worse than being unappreciated. Learn to be grateful for the big and little things your spouse does to make you feel loved, to lend a hand around the house, or to make your life more pleasant. Did he unload the dishwasher or fix something around the house? Did she wash and put away your clothes or prepare a delicious dinner? Many times we get busy and forget that the little things really are worth appreciating. Saying thank you can go a long way.

❤ *Take Action*: Tell your spouse how much you appreciate him or her and all they do for you. Write a note to your spouse thanking him or her for 10 things you appreciate, admire or enjoy about your spouse. For example, "Thank you for always kissing me goodbye. Thank you for taking care of yourself by going to the gym daily." Use beautiful stationery or colorful pens...make it artful or creative. Share your notes with each other.

48. Find Spirituality

Whether or not you believe in organized religion, find something to believe in together. Find something to have faith in. If you have different religions, respect the other's choice and share your beliefs without any pressure. If you do not have faith in any particular religion, research various religions together and find one that you might both find worthwhile. Educate yourselves and join a community of faith that supports your decision. You can live a spiritual life no matter what you believe. Find something to give you solace when times get tough. Find something to give you hope for your future. Whether you call it God, a Greater Power, All Mighty Being, chose to believe in something together to build a stronger marriage.

♥ *Take Action*: Try to find a common ground that brings you comfort in times of distress. Whether it is just learning to be grateful for what you have, praying or meditating together, or just finding joy in the present moment. You will find it comforting as a couple to have a shared belief. What do you believe in? Take the time to share your beliefs with your spouse.

49. Laugh Together

Laughter truly is the best medicine. Make sure your marriage is filled with laughter. It can come in many forms. You could go to a comedy club, you can tickle each other, you can rent a funny movie, or you can play charades. Ask your spouse, "What makes you laugh?" When is the last time you had a really good belly laugh with each other? Sometimes we get so serious that we forget to laugh. Laughter has many health benefits, including the release of endorphins. It is a great way to bond and can help you see the lighter side in life when things look a little grim. It's a great way to connect with your spouse in an intimate and silly way. Ha, ha, ha!

♥ *Take Action*: Make a list of things that make you laugh and schedule some laughter activities into your week.

This week I will laugh by doing the following with my spouse...

1. _____

2. _____

3. _____

4. _____

5. _____

6. _____

7. _____

8. _____

9. _____

50. Don't Read Minds

Don't expect your spouse to know what you need and want. And don't try to expect him or her to read your mind. Express your wants and desires. Do you want flowers for Valentine's Day?? Ask for them! He might think you don't want them because it's too traditional or expected. Do you wish she would ask you before making plans to go out with her friends? Tell her! She might not realize that you wanted some time alone with her. What have you got to lose by sharing what you want? Ask you spouse, "What can I do for you to be the best spouse I can be? What do you need from me?" You might be surprised at how easy it is to fulfill the needs of your spouse.

♥ *Take Action*: Make a list of what you'd like from your spouse. Share your lists with each other. In case you are not good at asking for what you want, here are some examples to get you started.

I would love it if you would…

1. Surprise me with a bouquet of flowers

2. Not leave your dirty laundry all over the floor

3. Snuggle me as we fall asleep at night

4. Tell me what you want sexually

5. Plan a romantic night out for us

6. Help me with paying the bills

7. Kiss me more often

8. Hold my hand as we walk down the street

9. Let me watch sports when I want to

About the Author

As a nationally published journalist, Sharael Kolberg has been writing for various magazines, newspapers and Web sites for nearly 20 years. Her work has appeared in publications such as *Outside* magazine, *Sunset Magazine* and *Working Woman* magazine. She has a B.A. in journalism from the University of Hawaii.

Sharael is also the author of her memoir, "Six Seasons Down Under: 45 Weeks of Adventures in Sydney and Beyond." Find out more about Sharael's work at www.sharael.com.

Sharael and her husband Jeff have been happily married for 14 years and enjoy raising their daughter in Orange County, CA.

www.ingramcontent.com/pod-product-compliance
Lightning Source LLC
Chambersburg PA
CBHW071817020426
42331CB00007B/1522